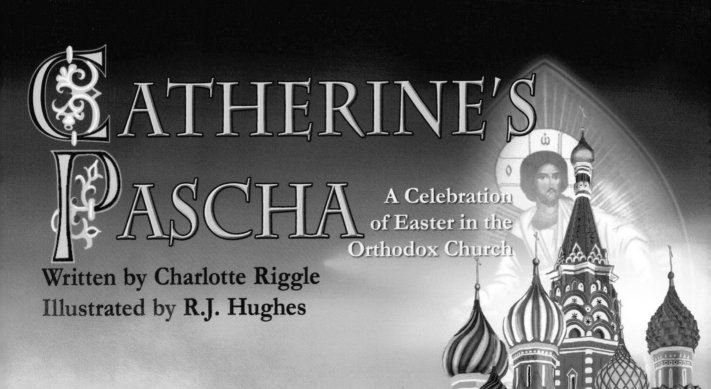

Catherine's Pascha

Pascha

A Celebration of Easter in the Orthodox Church

Written by Charlotte Riggle

Illustrated by R.J. Hughes

Many thanks to the Very Reverend Fathers John Troy Mashburn, Michael Oleksa, and Jerome Cwiklinski and the Reverend Fathers Marty Watt and Joseph Bittle, who helped us ensure that the liturgical and ecclesial details were right. Any errors that remain are entirely the fault of the author.

CATHEDRAL OF VASILY THE BLESSED; Собор Василия Блаженного; *"Saint Basil's Cathedral"*; Moscow, Russia; 1561

For Mary Elizabeth, who grew up long before the book was done

-C.R

For my own beloved daughters

-R.J.H

Thank You to Jennifer Harshman, Trent Terry, Mickey Hodges, Tracy Thallas, Danielle Wiegel, Evelyn Nicholas, Dr. Larry Helyer, Ben Greenhoe, and Sarah Fountain, for all the help you gave this project through your amazing variety of talents and skills.

Most especially, Alex Riggle and Justin Hughes, for your joy in our work, your tolerance of neglected chores, your willingness to accept the cost of this project, in dollars and time and attention, and your unflagging encouragement, enthusiasm, and support.

To all of you, and to everyone who helped us and whom we failed to acknowledge through ignorance, forgetfulness, or the multitude of names: Thank you!

Published by Phoenix Flair Press

Printed in the United States of America

ISBN: 978-0-9846124-3-7

catherinespascha.com

Mom says I have to go to bed at my regular time, even though it's Holy Saturday.

"But, Mom!" I say. "It's going to be time to get up in just a little while!"

"All the more reason for you to get a little nap," she says, and she turns off the light.

Well, Mom can make me go to bed, but she can't make me go to sleep. I'm going to stay awake until it's time to go to church.

"Wake up, Catherine. It's time to go to church," says Dad.

I blink at the light and yawn. "I'm not sleeping," I say. "I'm ju[st] resting my eyes."

I get dressed quickly. Mom combs my hair.

"I already combed it!" I say. Mom combs it anyway.

Dad carries my little brother, Peter, to the car and buckles him into his seat. I carry his blanket and pillow.

Mom carries the Pascha baskets. One of them is full of little ham and cheese sandwiches. The other one has sticky sweet rolls shaped like bunnies. Mom only makes them at Pascha. They're the best.

"Don't you want a blanket?" Mom asks.

"No," I say. "I'm going to stay awake the whole time."

...FOR THE ENEMY, HADES, HATH BEEN DESPOILED;

LET CREATION REJOICE, LET ALL THAT ARE BORN OF EARTH BE GLAD...

...AND ON THE THIRD DAY...

The church is dark. Dad puts our basket on the steps by the icons. Mom si[ts] down with my brother in her lap. I get to hold the candles.

"Blessed is our God," sings Father Nicholas as the service begins. I loo[k] around for the tomb. It's up by the icons. At Grandma's church last yea[r] the tomb was still in the middle when we got to church.

"Mom," I whisper. "When is Father Nicholas going to take the shroud ou[t] of the tomb?"

CATHEDRAL OF CHRIST THE SAVIOUR

LET THE WOMEN COME WITH MYRRH TO MEET ME...

Do not weep for me,

...FOR I AM DELIVERING ADAM AND EVE WITH ALL THEIR OFFSPRING...

for I shall arise and be glorified

...I SHALL RISE AGAIN.

"The shroud isn't in the tomb, sweetheart. It's already on the altar."

"At Grandma's church last year, the priest took the shroud out of the tomb."

"Oh, of course," Mom whispers. "That was beautiful, wasn't it? They do things a little bit differently at Grandma's church."

I'm not sure I want things to be different. I like it when things are the same. And I really liked it when the priest lifted up the shroud.

Храм Христа Спасителя; Moscow, Russia; 1883, 2000

COME RECEIVE THE LIGHT...

...Who Is Risen...

After a little while, Father Nicholas brings a candle out. "Com
and receive the Light," he sings. I love this part!

HOLY RESURRECTION CATHEDRAL 復活大

...THAT IS NEVER OVERTAKEN BY NIGHT...

...AND GLORIFY CHRIST...

...FROM THE DEAD.

Father Nicholas lights the candles of the people in the front. Then other people light candles from theirs. And then it's my turn.

聖堂 "NIKOLAI-DO" TOKYO, JAPAN 1891

...THE ANGELS SING IN THE HEAVENS;

THY RESURRECTION O CHRIST SAVIOR...

I light my candle, then I look around. The church is full of ligh

And then the choir starts to sing "Thy Resurrection, O Christ our Savior, the angels in heaven sing," and we follow Father Nicholas and the choir out the door of the church.

TRINITY CHURCH Церковь Святой Троицы
King George Island, Antarctica; 2005

...ENABLE US ON EARTH...

...TO GLORIFY THEE IN PURITY OF HEART

My candle blows out, and I stop to relight it from Elizabeth's candle. Elizabeth is my best friend.

Then Elizabeth's candle blows out, so she relights hers from mine.

HOLY RESURRECTION CHURCH
Kodiak Island, Alaska, USA; 1796

ROLLED AWAY-FOR IT WAS VERY LARGE. AND ENTERING T...

WHEN THEY LOOKED UP, THEY SAW THAT THE STONE HAD BEEN

...BUT HE SAID TO THEM, "DO NOT BE ALARMED. YOU SEE

When we get to the front of the church, we stand in the yard while Father Nicholas reads the Gospel. Mom holds Peter's candle so he won't catch someone's hair on fire.

CHURCH OF THE HOLY SEPULCHRE

JESUS OF NAZARETH, WHO WAS CRUCIFIED. *HE IS RISEN!"*

The wind makes me shiver.

"I'm cold," Peter says.

"Shh," I say. "It's the Gospel."

JERUSALEM, 325 AD

...WHICH THE LORD

THIS IS THE DAY...

... AND BE GLAD

Then Father Nicholas bangs on the door with his cross and shouts, "Lift up your gates so the King of Glory can come in."

A voice from inside shouts back, "Who is the King of Glory?" The voice sounds familiar. I look around for my dad.

Father Nicholas bangs and shouts again. "Lift up your gates so the King of Glory can come in."

THE GREAT CHURCH, HAGIA SOPHIA

HATH   MADE...

...LET US REJOICE...

IN IT 〜 PS. 118:24.

Again the voice says, "Who is the King of Glory?"

"Mom," I whisper, "is that Dad?"

"Shh," she says.

Father Nicholas bangs and shouts again. "Lift up your gates so the King of Glory can come in."

"Who is the King of Glory?"

Μεγάλη Ἐκκλησία Ἁγία Σοφία, 360 AD

TRAMPLING DOWN

CHRIST IS RISEN FROM THE DEAD,

BESTOWING

"The Lord of Hosts! He is the King of Glory!" shouts Father Nicholas. Then the door is thrown open and the big bell rings.

"Christ is risen from the dead!" we sing as we go back in. It's bright inside.

CHURCH OF SAINT GEORGE; القديس جورج
BUILT ABOVE AN OLDER CHURCH (POSSIBLY

DEATH BY DEATH,

AND UPON THOSE IN THE TOMBS

LIFE! ✦

I see Dad come down the aisle toward us.

"That was you inside, wasn't it?" I say.

"Shh," he says.

كنيسة OLD CAIRO, EGYPT; 900 -999 AD;
AN OLDER ST. GEORGE) ESTABLISHED 684 AD

...LET US BE RADIANT, O YE PEOPLE;

IT IS THE DAY OF RESURRECTION,

...CHRIST GOD HATH BROUGHT US...

My mom and Elizabeth's mom let us sit together. During the litany, I drip wax onto my fingers. It's hot, and it stings a little, but it looks neat.

Mom says we'll burn ourselves or catch our hair on fire so she makes us blow our candles out. I give her my sad look, but she doesn't notice.

CHURCH OF THE HOLY TRINITY AT THE LAVRA MAMBRE MONASTE
IGLESIA DE LA SANTÍSIMA TRINIDAD   Lake Amatitlan, Guatemala; 2007

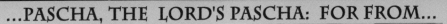

...PASCHA, THE LORD'S PASCHA: FOR FROM...

...DEATH TO LIFE, AND FROM EARTH TO HEAVEN,

...AS WE SING THE SONG OF VICTORY.

And then I hear the bells! The little bells on the censers were gone during Lent, and they're back! The choir is singing, and the bells are jingling, and the priest censes all the way around the church.

"Christ is risen!" he shouts. "Indeed, he is risen!" we all shout back.

Then he shouts it in Greek: "Christos anesti!" "Alithos anesti!" we all shout. I shout louder than Elizabeth.

ST. SPYRIDON AND CHURCH OF THE RESURRECTION; Ἅγιος Σπυρίδων Ἐκκλησία και η Εκκλησία της Αναστάσεως ;   Oia, Santorini, Greece; ca. 1860 - 1910

FOR BEHOLD, LIKE BEACONS SHEDDING LIGHT

LIFT YOUR EYES AROUND YOU, SION, AND SEE

BLESSING CHRIST IN YOU

"Khristos voskrese!" he shouts. "Voistinu voskrese!" we all shout. Elizabeth shou[ts] louder than me. Sometimes I can't remember how to say it in Russian.

We all sing, "Christ is risen from the dead, trampling down death by death, and upo[n] those in the tombs, bestowing life!" And then there are some prayers, and then it's th[e] deacon's turn to cense all the way around.

"Christ is risen!" the deacon shouts. "Indeed, he is risen!" we all shout back.

He shouts in Arabic: "Al Massieh kam!" "Hakkan kam!" we all shout.

ST. GEORGE'S CHURCH; IGREJA ORTODOXA SÃO JORGE; Brasilia, Brazil; 1994

DIVINE YOUR CHILDREN HAVE COME TO YOU, FROM WEST AND NORTH, FROM THE SEA AND FROM THE EAST

TO ALL THE AGES!

Then in Spanish: "Cristo ha resucitado!" "En verdad ha resucitado!"

The deacon slows down near the family from Alaska. "Kristuussaaq Unguirtuq!" he shouts.

Elizabeth and I look at each other. We practiced the Yup'ik together. "Ilumun Unguirtuq!" we shout as loud as we can.

It's hot in the church. Peter has gone to sleep on the bench. "Wake up, Peter! You'll miss Pascha!" I say. "Shhh," Mom says. I don't know how Peter can sleep. I'm not a bit sleepy.

ANNUNCIATION GREEK ORTHODOX CHURCH
Wauwatosa, Wisconsin, USA; 1961

...REMEMBER ALL OF YOU

MAY THE LORD GOD...

...AND TO THE

MARIAMITE CATHEDRAL OF DAMASCUS;

IN HIS KINGDOM...

...NOW AND FOREVER...

AGES OF AGES

الكنيسة المريمية Damascus, Syria; ca. 100 - 200 A.D

Χριστὸς ἀνέστη ἐκ νεκρῶν, θανάτῳ θάνατον πατήσας

CHRIST IS RISEN FROM THE DEAD. TRAMPLING DOWN DEATH BY DEATH,...

Христос воскресе из мертвых, смертию смерть

"Come on, Catherine, wake up" says Mom. "It's time to tak[e] Communion."

"I know," I say. "I'm not sleeping. I'm just resting my eyes."

There are so many, many people, it seems like it takes forever fo[r] everyone to receive Communion. I want the service to go faster now[.] It's almost time for the feast!

CATHEDRAL OF THE MOST HOLY TRINITY ; *CATEDRAL ORTODOXA RUSA DE LA SANTÍSIMA TRINIDAD*; Buenos Aires, Argentina, 1901

καὶ τοῖς ἐν τοῖς μνήμασι, ζωὴν χαρισάμενος!

...AND UPON THOSE IN THE TOMBS BESTOWING LIFE!

поправ, и сущим во гробех живот даровав!

At the end of the service, Father Nicholas shouts, "Christ is risen!"

"Indeed, He is risen!" we all shout again.

Then Father Nicholas prays and blesses all the baskets of food with holy water. I wish I could get closer to the baskets. Then maybe I would get blessed with the holy water too.

SAINT ELIJAH SERBIAN ORTHODOX CHURCH; *"Sveti Ilija"*;
Coober Pedy, South Australia, Australia, 1992

"Sweetie, not yet, you have to wait for everyone."

"Chicken!"

"Oh! You smell that?"

"I want hot dogs!"

"Mom's right behind us, Phoebe.

Mom carries our baskets downstairs to the fellowship hall. The tables are already full of ham and bacon, deviled eggs, sausage biscuits, sweet bread and paska cheese, cookies, baklava — and hot dogs! Somebody brought hot dogs!

Dad puts my little brother on his blanket in the Sunday school room

THE CHURCH OF OUR LADY MARY OF ZION ርዕሰ አድባራ

"Gonna need a place on the table for the roast!"

"An omlet in a bread bowl? How do you make that?"

Let's find a table while we wait for her."

"Peter, there's hot dogs!" I tell him.

"Shh," says Dad. "He can have a hot dog tomorrow."

"Do I have to eat vegetables?" I ask.

"No, Catherine. Tonight you can have anything you want."

ቅድስተ ቅዱሳን ድንግል ማርያም ፅዮን   Axum, Ethiopia; ca. 336-400 AD

"Can I have all desserts, Mom?"   "No"

"That roast is going quick–save me a piece?"

"Oooh! paska cheese!"   "Is there summer sausag

I put two hot dogs on my plate, with a sticky bunny, five chocolate kisses, cheese curls, an oatmeal cookie, and a big piece of chocolate cake. Then I get a red egg.

SAINT SOPHIA'S CATHEDRAL,

"But we ate only veggies for..forever!"

"Did Andrea bring her bacon-wrapped dates this year?"

and crackers, too? I've been craving those."

Elizabeth gets fried chicken instead of hot dogs, but everything else is just the same.

London, England, 1882

"What? I got a real one this year!" "Like the 'real wood' eg

"Hey there, Nick!" "Oh No Uncle Gus, not the old wood egg again!"

"I don't even have the wood one anymore!

I bang eggs with Elizabeth. Hers breaks. Then I bang eggs with Mom. Hers breaks, too.

"Hooray!" I say. "I've got the luckiest egg!"

ALL SAINTS CHURCH AT ST. NICHOLAS SEMINARY
ALL SAINTS CHURCH KATIKA SAINT NICHOLAS SEMINARI; **Kasikizi, Tanzania; 2004**

ast year ... and the year before?"   "It's a real, actual egg!"

"Sorry Uncle Gus, I'm not falling for that... again"

...cause I gave it to your cousin"

Then Elizabeth and I get more chocolate kisses and I get another sticky bunny. We sit by the edge of the stage to eat and talk.

I'm warm and full and happy, but I'm still not a bit sleepy.

HOLY LIFE-GIVING TRINITY ORTHODOX CHURCH
คริสตศาสนจักรออร์โธด็อกซ์แห่งพระตรีเอกานุภาพ   **Phuket, Thailand; 2011**

GREEK: Χριστὸς ἀνέστη! Ἀληθῶς ἀνέστη!

HEBREW: ‏המשיח קם! באמת קם!‏

CHRIST IS RISEN!   INDEED HE IS RISEN!

Soon Dad says it's time to go home.
"Christ is risen!" we say to our friends as we leave.
"Indeed He is risen!" they say. "Good night!"

HOLY TRINITY GREEK ORTHODOX CATHEDRAL
New Orleans, Louisiana, USA; 1864

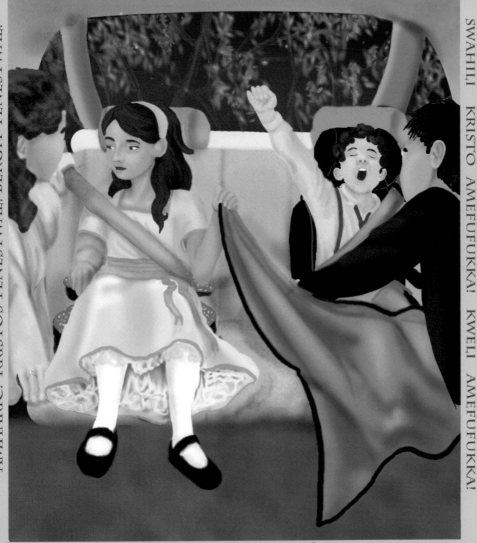

MAORI: KUA ARA A TE KARAITI ; HE PONO TONU, KUA ARA A IA

SWAHILI KRISTO AMEFUFUKKA! KWELI AMEFUFUKKA!

OLD CHURCH SLAVONIC: Христо́съ воскрЕ́се! Воистину воскресе!

"Good night, Mom," I say. "Can I use Peter's blanket?"

"Why? You're not sleepy, are you?" she asks.

"No," I say. "I'm not sleepy. I just want to rest my eyes."

She tucks the blanket around me and kisses my forehead. "Christ is risen!" she says.

"Indeed He is risen!" I say. "Good night."

ST. DEMETRIOS GREEK ORTHODOX CHURCH
Winnipeg, Manitoba, Canada; 1958

SACRED MONASTERY OF THE GOD-TRODDEN MOUNT SINA
Ιερά Μονή Θεοβαδίστου Όρους Σινά

"I ... missed ... Pascha!"

"SAINT CATHERINE'S MONASTERY" Sinai, Egypt: ca. 565 AD

The Words We Use

Depending on your background, there may be words in *Catherine's Pascha* that are unfamiliar to you, or that you don't know how to pronounce.

The word Pascha, our word for Easter, is said *PAH-ska*.

The Paschal greeting, *Christ is risen,* and the response, *Indeed, he is risen,* might be a little harder to say in languages you're unfamiliar with. If you use this guide, you'll be close enough:

In Greek: Christos anesti: *khree-STOHSS ah-NES-tee*

                  Alithos anesti: *ah-lee-THOHSS ah-NES-tee*

In Russian: Khristos voskrese: *khree-STOHSS voh-SKRES*

                  Voistinu voskrese: *voh-EE-stee-noo voh-SKRES*

In Arabic: Al Massieh kam: *el me-SEE-eh KAM*

                  Hakkan kam: *A-ken KAM*

In Spanish: Cristo ha resucitado: *KREE-sto ah reh-soo-see-TAH-do*

                  En verdad ha resusitado: *en ver-DAHD ah reh-soo-see-TAH-do*

In Yup'ik: Kristuussaaq Unguirtuq: *kris-TOO-sahk ung-WEK-tohk*

                  Ilumun Unguirtuq: *ee-LOO-men ung-WEK-tohk*

Those unfamiliar with Orthodox worship may find these brief definitions helpful:

Cense: To bless something with the smoke from burning incense

Censer: A container used to hold burning incense

Communion: Bread and wine that are consecrated and received as an act of Christian worship; also called *Eucharist.*

Gospel: The first four books of the New Testament, bound together in a single volume and kept on the altar, or a reading from one of these four books

Icon: A stylized picture of a saint or of an event from the Bible or the life of a saint

Litany: A series of prayers offered by the priest or deacon, with set responses (most often, "Lord, have mercy") by the people

Shroud: An embroidered cloth icon showing Christ's body removed from the Cross and being prepared for burial

Tomb: An intricately carved and decorated wooden bier that represents the tomb in which Christ was buried

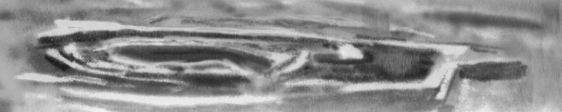

CHURCH OF THE SEVEN APOSTLES OVERLOOKING TH
CENTURY HOUSE CHURCH BELIEVED TO BE ST PETER'S
Archaeological site now sheltered beneath St Peter's Memorial (Church); 1990

Frequently Asked Questions

Pascha! It is by far the most important day of the year, and the biggest celebration, in the Orthodox Church. If you're not familiar with the celebration of Pascha, though, you may have some questions. If you don't see the answers you're looking for here, check out our website, **www.catherinespascha.com.**

There you'll find even more about Pascha, along with recipes for Pascha treats, the history of the churches depicted in this book, activity sheets and study guides for children, and lots more.

Why do you call Easter Pascha?

The earliest Christians called the feast *Pesach*, the Hebrew word for Passover, because the Passover was being celebrated when Jesus was raised from the dead. Pesach was adapted into Greek as *Pascha*. As the Christian faith spread throughout the world, the Greek word was adapted into other languages. So, if you speak Spanish, you call the feast *Pascua*; if you speak French, *Pâques*; if Danish, *Påske*.

When Christianity was embraced by the English people, though, Pascha always fell during the month they called *Eosturmonath*. Over time, they began to call the feast by the name of the month, and so the feast is called *Easter* by most people in the English-speaking world.

Why is the Pascha service in the middle of the night?

As with so many of life's interesting questions, there's a simple answer, and a complicated answer. The simple answer is that Christ was raised in the middle of the night, and we don't see any reason to wait for the sun to come up. At the very first moment of Pascha, at the very beginning of the day of the Resurrection, we begin the celebration! If that were the only answer, it would be enough. But there's more to it than that. The complicated answer has to do with chronos and kairos, clock time and God's time. If you want that answer, you'll find it on our website, **www.catherinespascha.com.**

Why did Catherine want hot dogs?

Orthodox Christians prepare for Pascha with many weeks of fasting and prayer. During these weeks, called Lent, we don't eat meat or other animal products. When Pascha finally comes, we enjoy all the foods we've fasted from. Adults often look forward to having favorite foods like ham or bacon or lamb. Catherine looked forward to having her favorite food, too. Her favorite is hot dogs.

Why was the Pascha service different at Catherine's grandmother's church?

The Orthodox Church is very, very old. And over the centuries, as the Church spread throughout the world, Orthodox Christians in different places developed different customs to express the faith they all shared. When Orthodox Christians first came to America, they brought their customs and traditions from their homelands. Parishes that were started by immigrants from the Middle East, like Catherine's parish, had one set of customs, and parishes that were started by immigrants from Slavic countries, like Catherine's grandmother's parish, had different customs. Over time, as Orthodox Christians from different backgrounds began to worship together, old customs blended in new and beautiful ways. As a result, when you go to a Pascha service, your experience may be different from Catherine's. There may be red eggs, or intricately decorated pysanky eggs, or no eggs at all. Pascha baskets may be blessed in the nave, or on the church porch, or in the fellowship hall. It's even possible that the service might be in the morning rather than in the middle of the night! But whenever and however Pascha is celebrated, the joy in the Resurrection of Christ will be the same, as will be our joyous shout:

CHRIST IS RISEN! INDEED HE IS RISEN!

RUINS OF A BYZANTINE CHURCH COVERING A FIRST
Capernaum, Galilee, Israel; 1931; ca. 450 AD; ca. First Century AD.

CPSIA information can be obtained at www.ICGtesting.com
Printed in the USA
BVIW12n2008190315
392000BV00001B/1